THEATRE CENTRE

by **Mohamed-Zain Dada**

Dizzy was commissioned by Theatre Centre and is a co-production between Theatre Centre and Sheffield Theatres.

Dizzy premiered at Tanya Moiseiwitsch Playhouse at Sheffield Theatres on Wednesday 25 September 2024.

by Mohamed-Zain Dada

CAST
QAMAR — **Sera Mustafa**
STAX — **Brendan Barclay**
YASEEN — **Reda Elazouar**

CREATIVES
Director and Dramaturg — **Rob Watt**
Designer — **Hannah Sibai**
Movement Director — **Yami Löfvenberg**
Sound Designer & Soundscape Composer — **Mwen**
Lighting Designer — **Jess Brigham**

PRODUCTION
Marketing for Theatre Centre — **Rachel Bellman**
Graffiti Consultant — **Cherry Bee**
Producers for Theatre Centre — **Rowan Blake Prescott and Emma Rees**

Company Stage Manager — **Lizzie Bond**
Teacher Resource Writer — **Susie Ferguson**
Schools Tour Booking — **Becky Ide**
PR — **Storytelling PR / Jo Allan PR**

Marketing Consultants — **Jane Morgan Associates**
Casting Consultant — **Becky Paris**
Artwork — **Rebecca Pitt**
Production Manager — **Herbe Walmsley**

THEATRE CENTRE

Founded in 1953 by Brian Way and Margaret Faulks, we've been a vital catalyst for youth leadership and creativity for seventy years.

In this time, we've commissioned 108 writers and produced 237 plays. We have played to audiences of over one million in schools and theatres and we have worked with over 250,000 young people through a vast range of projects. Some of those young people are now working in the arts, running companies of their own, or in education teaching drama to the next generations.

We commission new writing from trailblazing writers, touring directly into schools and theatres UK-wide, as well as running our year-round Future Makers activities to bring young people, artists, and teachers together as creative collaborators. Future Makers makes space for young people to have agency as they nurture their talent and interests on their terms.

We see access, equality, and representation as foundations of a fair society and work to dismantle exclusion and systemic injustice. We prioritise areas that are systemically underserved and excluded, removing economic and social barriers, and working where young people can benefit most. We celebrate the true creative diversity only the widest access can bring.

THEATRE CENTRE TEAM

Marketing Manager **Rachel Bellman**
Programme & Administration Coordinator **Grace Lambert**
Finance Manager **David Lewis**
Producer **Rowan Blake Prescott**
Executive Director & CEO **Emma Rees**
Artistic Director **Rob Watt**
www.theatre-centre.co.uk

Dizzy was created through conversations with hundreds of young people across the UK. We would particularly like to thank the following young people who made a significant contribution:

Aliyah Chaumoo, Arthur Thorpe, Barnaby Mosley, Eireann Devlin, Elliot Goodhill, Francesca McBride, Georgie Dettmer, Grace Lambert, Gracie Oddie-James, Imogen Denham, Isabella Lawrence, Isabelle Searle, Jai Britto, James Leggot, James Malam, Jasmine Clarke, Liubov Manzarkhanova, Lucy Munday, Maryam Shahabuddin, Paige Newman, Phoebe Long-Soday, Rana Bada, Rhys Heal, Rojin Haddadzadegan, Sam Wolffe and Zihora Onwuka.

We would also like to thank the following partners:

Addey and Stanhope School, Lewisham; Creative Crawley; Creative Village; Hazelwick School, Crawley; National Youth Theatre; Newfield School, Sheffield, Parkside Community School, Chesterfield.

Amanda and David Binks.

Rob Hastie.

Backstage Trust and John Thaw Foundation for their support of Future Makers and the Garrick Trust for their support of our Resident Writers, all of which were crucial in the development of *Dizzy*. Everyone who supported our The Big Give, Arts for Impact campaign.

Our Chair, Rebecca Major, and Trustees, Aleksa Asme, James Cooney, Titilola Dawudu, Benjamin Eva-Griffiths, Romana Flello, Frazer Flintham, Joanne Leung, Kieran Lines, David Luff, Karl Singporewala and Caroline Wilkes.

SHEFF!ELD THEATRES

Sheffield Theatres is home to three theatres: the Crucible, the Sheffield landmark with a world-famous reputation; the Playhouse, an intimate, versatile space for getting closer to the action; and the gleaming Lyceum, the beautiful proscenium that hosts the best of the UK's touring shows.

Having held the title 'Regional Theatre of the Year' on four separate occasions, Sheffield Theatres is the ticket to big names and local heroes, timeless treasures and new voices. Committed to investing in the creative leaders of the future, Sheffield Theatres' dedicated talent development hub, The Bank, supports a new cohort of emerging theatre-makers every year.

Sheffield Theatres has a reputation for bold new work. Starting life in the Crucible in 2019, the award-winning *Life of Pi* transferred to the West End in 2021 and to Broadway in 2023, returning home to Sheffield Theatres to launch its 2023–24 UK and Ireland tour. This success follows hit musical *Everybody's Talking About Jamie* which also transferred to the West End, toured the UK and enjoyed a feature film release internationally on Amazon Prime in 2021. *Everybody's Talking About Jamie* returned to Sheffield on tour in 2024. In 2022, *Rock/Paper/Scissors* was staged across all three theatres to celebrate the fiftieth anniversary of the Crucible and Playhouse, winning Best Directors at the UK Theatre Awards that year. Also during the anniversary year, the acclaimed *Accidental Death of an Anarchist* opened the newly named Tanya Moiseiwitsch Playhouse in September 2022. The show transferred to the West End in June 2023, winning a UK Theatre Award in the same year. Over Christmas 2022, Sheffield Theatres, in co-production with the National Theatre and Various Productions, revived *Standing at the Sky's Edge*, returning the show to the Crucible before transferring to the Olivier Theatre and winning two Olivier awards including Best New Musical. The show transferred to the West End in February 2024. In 2023, Sheffield Theatres' productions received five UK Theatre Award nominations, including two for their reimagined revival of *Miss Saigon*, staged by special arrangement with Cameron Mackintosh in summer 2023.

SHEFFIELD THEATRES TEAM

Chief Executive **Tom Bird**

Deputy Chief Executive **Bookey Oshin**

Crucible Lyceum Playhouse 55 Norfolk Street, Sheffield, S1 1DA

sheffieldtheatres.co.uk

Sheffield Theatres Crucible Trust is a Registered Charity. No. 1120640 and is a company limited by guarantee No. 6035820

DIZZY

Mohamed-Zain Dada

With original artwork by Cherry Bee

THIS THING HERE IS A CLASH OF CLASS,
LOOKING AT THE AFTERMATH
AFTER OUR KID PASSED
LIKE I'M NOT SURE WHERE TO START.

THEY SAY ARTISTS NEVER REALLY DIE
I WROTE HIS NAME SO I DIDN'T CRY
I SAY I'M OK BUT THAT'S A LIE,
I WROTE HIS NAME I HAD TO TRY.

DIZZY THIS DIZZY THAT
I JUST WANNA SEE DIZZY BACK.
I PAINT WHITE FILLS & THE OUTLINES BLACK.
I GOT THE CITY UNDER ATTACK
ALL I HEAR IS DIZZY THIS DIZZY THAT.

ARTISTS NEVER REALLY DIE
I WROTE HIS NAME SO I DIDN'T CRY
I SAY I'M OK THAT'S A LIE,
I WROTE HIS NAME I HAD TO TRY.

MOHAMED-ZAIN DADA

Mohamed-Zain Dada, who goes by the name Zain, is a playwright and screenwriter. His first writing credit, *Emily (Glitched) In Paris* was for the Royal Court Theatre's Living Newspaper series in March 2021.

He is also an alumnus of BBC Drama Room's 2022–23 cohort and NFTS x Left Bank Pictures inaugural Diverse Writer's Room Programme 2024. Zain's debut play *Blue Mist* premiered at the Jerwood Theatre Upstairs at the Royal Court Theatre in October 2023 to a sold-out run, four- and five-star reviews, and was nominated for an Olivier Award.

CHERRY BEE

Cherry Bee is a London-born artist whose work with colour and space, crossed with his knowledge of graffiti, has made his mark on the city – and has led to him working with the likes of Drake, The Weeknd and many more.

Instagram/TikTok: cherrybeearts

During the course of writing this play, I commissioned a graffiti mural in Shepherd's Bush, West London, in honour of Palestinian poet Heba Abu Nada (24 June 1991–20 October 2023). The artwork is by Captain Kris (@captainkris) in partnership with Creative Debuts.

The mural includes an excerpt from Heba's poem, 'Not Just Passing' (translated by Huda Fakhreddine), which was first published in English in *Arablit Quarterly* on 28 November 2023.

> *You were first created out of love,*
> *so carry nothing but love*
> *to those who are trembling.*

Heba Abu Nada was a Palestinian poet, novelist, and educator. Her novel الأكسجين ليس للموتى (*Oxygen is Not for the Dead*) won second place in the Sharjah Award for Arab Creativity in 2017. She was killed in her home in the Gaza Strip by an Israeli airstrike on 20 October 2023. She was thirty-two.

Huda Fakhreddine is Associate Professor of Arabic literature at the University of Pennsylvania. She is a writer, a translator, and the author of several scholarly books.

Acknowledgements

Thank you to Rob Watt for believing in this play from the very beginning. For holding this process with care, commitment and a collaborative spirit. To Rachel Taylor for your brilliant notes. To Gurnesha Bola for your dramaturgical support and encouragement every step of the way.

To the brilliant company: actors Sera Mustafa, Brendan Barclay and Reda Elazouar. To Lizzie Bond, Mwen, Hannah Sibai, Jess Brigham, Yami Löfvenberg, Herbe Walmsley, Becky Paris and Rebecca Pitt. And everyone at Theatre Centre, Sheffield Theatres and Nick Hern Books.

Special thanks to my parents, Fehmida and Ashraf Dada, and my siblings, Zara Al Akku, Nadia Dada, Humzah Al Akku and Nadir Dada. To Barney Clark and Cherry Bee for giving me an insight into the world of graffiti writers with such openness and love. And to all the young people in schools, youth centres and youth groups across England who helped to inform and shape each draft of this play.

M-Z.D., 2024

Characters

QAMAR, *fifteen, Arab*
STAX / SUNNY, *thirty-three*
YASEEN / DIZZY, *eighteen, Arab*
MR KADINSKY
SECURITY GUARD

In the *Axis* scenes, an (*Echo*) indicates a voice from the past, present and future.

Setting

The action of the play is set across several locations – each encapsulated by its sonic landscape with the sound of trains rattling by, cars along a dual carriageway or the store announcements of a paint shop.

Note

Dashes (–) at the beginnings and ends of lines of dialogue are intended to be slight pauses or a shift to a different train of thought.

This text went to press before the end of rehearsals and so may differ slightly from the play as performed.

ACT ONE

Scene One

Somewhere, someplace. The Axis. QAMAR *is in a hypnotic state.*

QAMAR One foot, in front of the other.

Second to second.

Minute to minute.

Hour to hour.

Inch by inch.

No sense of rhythm.

No sense of time.

Things float by.

Pass by.

Sleepwalking into the present.

Scene Two

A wall which now functions as a memorial with a small bouquet of flowers. A man in a mask, STAX, *looks around, takes out a spray can and starts tagging the wall.*

QAMAR *enters. She takes her phone out and starts filming.* STAX, *is oblivious.*

QAMAR Smile for the camera, criminal.

STAX *turns around.*

STAX   What do you think you're doing?

QAMAR   What do you think I'm doing?

They circle each other.

STAX   Put that away.

QAMAR   No.

STAX   I'm serious.

QAMAR   I am documenting a CRIME.

STAX   Who do you think you are, Ross Kemp?

QAMAR   Won't be so funny locked behind bars.

STAX   What's the crime?

QAMAR   Vandalism.

STAX   You wanna see a real criminal –

QAMAR   – Defacing a wall –

STAX   – go to Canary Wharf –

QAMAR   – A wall that is special to me –

STAX   – Just put it down, for God's sake.

QAMAR   Don't use God's name in vain.

STAX   You an evangelical or something?

QAMAR   Yes, yes, that's exactly what I am.

QAMAR points out her hijab.

STAX   That was a joke –

QAMAR   – A stupid criminal, I see. What are you meant to be?

The masked singer.

STAX   Oi, no need to get rude.

STAX gets closer.

ACT ONE, SCENE TWO 11

QAMAR I know Brazilian jiu-jitsu.

STAX Do you go around telling randoms you know how to fight?

STAX inches closer.

QAMAR I'm like the hijabi Khabib. You don't wanna mess with me.

STAX And I'm Prince Naz's step-brother.

QAMAR Don't underestimate me.

STAX You're brave, I'll give you that.

QAMAR No, no, no. It's not about bravery. It's about what's right.

STAX You don't understand who you're dealing with, do you?

QAMAR I have a clear idea.

STAX Do you?

STAX circles her.

QAMAR A man with zero morals.

I don't care what you do to me.

Keep circling. Go on, keep circling.

You clearly want both legs broken.

STAX I'm gonna ask you one last time. Hand it over.

QAMAR Y-y-you don't scare me.

STAX inches even closer.

Take one more step and I will call the p–

STAX suddenly lunges forward and tries to grab her phone.

– Oi. Oi. GET OFF ME.

STAX	Give me that.
QAMAR	No. OUCH. OUCH. YOU'RE INJURING A MINOR.
	STOP. I'LL SCREAM.
STAX	I WARNED YOU.
QAMAR	PAEDO. PAEDO. PAEDO ATTACKING ME. ASSAULT.

STAX *stops.*

STAX	I AM NOT A NONCE.

STAX *takes the mask off.*

QAMAR	Ha.
STAX	Alright, alright. Just delete the footage. Okay. Can't be having the feds on my case again.
QAMAR	You've got a warrant out against you or something?
STAX	I'm on tag.
QAMAR	Let me think about it… Hmm.
	How about… No.
STAX	What you gonna do with it?
QAMAR	Leak it on TikTok. Show what a dickhead you are.
STAX	A dickhead for doing graff?
QAMAR	No, a dickhead for –

He lunges forward again. They struggle over her phone.

STAX	– Give it here, snitch.
QAMAR	NO.
STAX	What the hell is this iron grip?
QAMAR	NEVER SURRENDER.

A train above rattles by, QAMAR *is momentarily distracted by the noise.*

STAX *manages to grab her phone.* QAMAR *holds her hand as if he hurt her.*

STAX There we go.

I don't wanna hurt you, I did tell you. Can't be filming strangers like that.

Scene Three

Somewhere, someplace. The Axis. A train rattles by.

QAMAR *is in a hypnotic state.*

QAMAR One foot, in front of the other.

Second to second.

Minute to minute.

Hour to hour.

Inch by inch.

Twenty-four hours. Things float by.

YASEEN Remember Imam Abdullah?

QAMAR Yaseen?

YASEEN When you snaked me to Baba after the lesson.

QAMAR Yas? Is that you?

YASEEN You were always their favourite.

QAMAR That's not true.

YASEEN Model student, maths whiz. Destined to be a doctor.

QAMAR	That's what Baba wants, not me. And I want to set the record straight, you're the one who cut Imam Abdullah's beard when he fell asleep.
YASEEN	'Cause he slapped your hand when you made a mistake.
QAMAR	(*Echo.*) Don't do it, Yas.
YASEEN	I'm gonna do it.

The sound of a man snoring. QAMAR *smiles at the memory.*

QAMAR	(*Echo.*) I'm telling Mama.
YASEEN	I'm doing this for you.
QAMAR	(*Echo.*) We're gonna get in trouble.
YASEEN	I'm getting the scissors.
QAMAR	You terrorised the poor man.
YASEEN	Fake news.
QAMAR	(*Echo.*) Don't. Mama will kill you.
YASEEN	Shut up will you.

The man snoring stops as if he's about to wake up.

QAMAR	(*Echo.*) Put the scissors away.
YASEEN	You're gonna get a slap, Wallah. Respect your elders.
QAMAR	I got receipts for all your antics.
YASEEN	Go on then.
QAMAR	Farting on purpose then going to do *wudhu* five times in an hour, reading the Qur'an to the tune of Bob the builder, putting SMARTIES in my mouth when Imam Abdullah wasn't looking.

YASEEN	I'm about to cut it, *bismillah*.
QAMAR	(*Echo*.) Ugh. Silly.
YASEEN	Trim done.
	YASEEN *is in fits of laughter.*
	My man has gone from East London Mosque to tech bro in Shoreditch.
QAMAR	(*Echo*.) You're seeing *Jahanam*.
STAX	(*Echo*.) What's the crime?
YASEEN	Do *dua* I go *Jannah*.
STAX	(*Echo*.) What's the crime?
QAMAR	Yas? Yas?
STAX	(*Echo*.) Who do you think you are, Ross Kemp?
QAMAR	Yaseen?
STAX	(*Echo*.) You there? Hello? Yo?

Scene Four

The memorial wall.

STAX	Hello? Khabib in a headscarf.
QAMAR	Where the hell is my phone?
	STAX *hands it over.* QAMAR *snatches it back.*
STAX	You went –
	STAX *whistles.*
	– For a bit.

QAMAR walks toward the bouquet to check it's correctly in place.

QAMAR — This isn't the end.

STAX Tell you one thing, most people are too scared to say anything.

QAMAR It's not the last time you'll hear from me.

STAX And then you get a kid like you, filming and snitching.

QAMAR I'm not a kid.

STAX Is this a new TikTok trend? Like that 'very demure, very mindful' bollocks.

QAMAR You're going to get what's coming to you.

STAX Country has gone to pot.

QAMAR In this life or the next.

STAX We did have happy slapping in our day.

QAMAR You're going to face the full force of the law.

STAX Nah, I'm confused.

QAMAR I'll be back.

QAMAR gets up to leave.

STAX Alright Arnold.

QAMAR Arnold?

STAX imitates Arnold Schwarzenegger in The Terminator.

STAX '*I'll be back.*'

…No? Nothing?

QAMAR looks confused.

STAX imitates Arnold Schwarzenegger in Predator.

'*Get to di choppa.*'

ACT ONE, SCENE FOUR   17

QAMAR   Are you having a breakdown?

STAX   *The Terminator*? *Predator*? Nah? Wow, you're proper, proper young.

QAMAR   I've got to get back home.

STAX   What's your story? You interning for BTP?

QAMAR   BTP?

STAX   British Transport Police.

QAMAR   No, but now I know who to ring.

STAX   And say what?

QAMAR   You assaulted me.

STAX   Give it a break.

QAMAR   Assaulted a teenage girl.

STAX   What the hell is wrong with you?

QAMAR   What is wrong with you? You don't see those flowers?

                 And you put some squiggly rubbish on it?

STAX   Squiggly?

QAMAR   Vomit on a wall.

                 You can't see it's a memorial?

                 STAX *looks at the flowers.*

STAX   I know it is.

QAMAR   You know it is, yet you did what you did.

STAX   It's called paying homage.

QAMAR   – What does –

                 QAMAR *looks at the wall.*

                 – Dizzy even mean?

STAX   He was my brother.

QAMAR	No.
STAX	What do you mean, no?
QAMAR	I think we're talking about different people because –
STAX	– The boy that fell –
QAMAR	– Someone fell fifty metres –
STAX	– Yeah, and died.
QAMAR	– passed away.
STAX	Once someone goes, they're immortal.
QAMAR	– And you're sullying his memory.
STAX	Sullying?
QAMAR	SULL-YI-NG. Are you high?
STAX	Wish I was.
QAMAR	Did you see it happen?
STAX	Nah, I couldn't really go –

QAMAR *looks up*.

QAMAR	– At this distance, it's unlikely he would have reached terminal velocity. But the likelihood of mortality increases with the distance…

…Unless he was pushed.

STAX *looks baffled*.

STAX	Did you know Diz?
QAMAR	Who?
STAX	Yaseen?

QAMAR *freezes*.

QAMAR	Yaseen? Yas is –

– was my older brother.

ACT ONE, SCENE FOUR 19

STAX	Shit. I didn't know. I had no clue. I never meant any disrespect –
QAMAR	– What I need to understand is whether there was any foul play.
STAX	Foul play?
QAMAR	The police have officially said he fell. But calculating speed, time and distance would mean –
STAX	– Course the pigs aren't looking into it.

QAMAR *turns to look at* STAX.

QAMAR	You think he didn't? Do you think someone pushed him?

QAMAR *walks towards* STAX.

STAX	I don't know –
QAMAR	– Do you know what happened?
STAX	Easy. All I know is, I don't believe nothing the authorities say.

QAMAR *turns away.*

QAMAR	Helpful, thank you.
STAX	They're programmed to lie… innit. these lot lie about everything… Iraq war and weapons of mass destruction, uni fees… COVID.

QAMAR *looks at* STAX *suspiciously.*

QAMAR	Your algorithm must be absolutely wild.
STAX	I ain't a conspiracist, but I'm telling you, these 5G towers are dodgy.
QAMAR	You're saying you knew Yas?

Beat.

STAX	Yaseen was the heartbeat of the city.

QAMAR	He didn't tell me he did this stuff.
STAX	He done 'Free Gaza' near Whitehall and almost got nicked.

Diz was a real Jedi.

QAMAR *smiles*.

Look, I had no clue who you were.

No harm, no foul?

STAX *puts his hand out.* QAMAR *shakes it. She takes another moment to look at the tag in honour of* DIZZY.

STAX *looks at the wall.*

Rest in paint, Diz.

Scene Five

Somewhere, someplace. The Axis. The distant sound of a police siren.

QAMAR *is in a classroom. The voice of* MR KADINSKY, *Qamar's maths teacher, echoes throughout the scene.*

MR KADINSKY	0, 1, 1, 2, 3, 5, 8, 13, 21, 34, 55, 89. What do we call this, Qamar?
QAMAR	The Fibonacci –
MR KADINSKY	144, 233, 377, 610 –
QAMAR	– The Fibonacci sequence, Mr Kadinksy.
MR KADINSKY	Which is?
QAMAR	It's when the number before is equal to the sum of the two preceding numbers.

ACT ONE, SCENE FIVE 21

MR KADINSKY   Why?

QAMAR   What do you mean, that's the answer?

MR KADINSKY   Why, why, why, why, why?

QAMAR   Stop asking me –

MR KADINSKY   – Why?

QAMAR   It's the answer.

MR KADINSKY   What is the logic?

QAMAR   I've explained it.

MR KADINSKY   Define a circumference?

QAMAR   The distance around a fixed point.

MR KADINSKY   The distance?

QAMAR   That's what I said.

MR KADINSKY   The radius?

QAMAR   The distance from the centre of the circle.

MR KADINSKY   The circumference of a circle, divide it twice by the radius and it is –

QAMAR   – It is 3.14.

MR KADINSKY   Whether it's the moon or a ferris wheel.

QAMAR   Always.

MR KADINSKY   Because?

QAMAR   Because there is always an answer.

MR KADINSKY   Because?

QAMAR   There is always a reason.

MR KADINSKY   Divine proportions.

QAMAR   It's never ending.

MR KADINSKY   *Kun Faya Kun.*

Beat.

YASEEN	It's irrational.
QAMAR	Yaseen?
YASEEN	Nah, it's all irrational.
QAMAR	You're back?
YASEEN	It don't make sense.
QAMAR	What doesn't?
YASEEN	Algebra.
QAMAR	It's just about using symbols instead of numbers.
YASEEN	All that X, Y, Z stuff. Nah.
QAMAR	There are variables, operators and constants.
YASEEN	Forget trigonometry.
QAMAR	There is always a constant.
YASEEN	Could never sit still.
QAMAR	What did you get again?

QAMAR *smiles*.

YASEEN	And then I got a U.
QAMAR	It's actually a one now.
YASEEN	Everyone says I don't get it, but I clocked it all.
QAMAR	Who doesn't?
YASEEN	They go harder on me bumping train than the guys in suits pressing the button.
QAMAR	Talk to me.
YASEEN	They throw us under the bus and tell us to act civilised when we get vexed.
QAMAR	What do you mean?

ACT ONE, SCENE FIVE

YASEEN   They tell us lot to rise above it.

QAMAR   Can you hear me?

YASEEN   But they don't even want to say our names when we're dead.

QAMAR   Where are you right now?

YASEEN   They can televise genocide and it's calm. Televise ethnic cleansing and it's calm.

QAMAR   Who is?

YASEEN   They keep on telling lies.

QAMAR   Yas?

YASEEN   But it ain't adding up.

QAMAR   Let me explain.

YASEEN   There is no sense in sense.

QAMAR   Let me help.

YASEEN   Not sure if I'm –

QAMAR   – Stop

QAMAR is desperate to escape the Axis.

YASEEN   – A shooting star.

QAMAR   – Stop now.

YASEEN   – Or a fiery asteroid.

QAMAR   I can't do this.

YASEEN   – Light up the sky –

QAMAR   I really can't.

YASEEN   – Or burn it all down.

Beat. A calm.

STAX   (*Echo.*) What do we call that?

YASEEN   A throw-up, Stax.

QAMAR	Who?
STAX	(*Echo*.) Good job.
QAMAR	Yas?
STAX	(*Echo*.) What's a burner?
YASEEN	A two-three colour piece.
STAX	(*Echo*.) Good job, Yaseen.
	Why?
YASEEN	Divine proportion, my bro.
STAX	(*Echo*.) The golden ratio.
YASEEN	The composition of that slaps, Stax.
STAX	(*Echo*.) Imagine seeing that on a moving bus.
YASEEN	Or a train.
STAX	(*Echo*.) Or on a building.
YASEEN	Or a narrow ledge. Tiptoeing to get it done.
STAX	(*Echo*.) Whatever it takes.
YASEEN	To get your name in lights.
STAX	(*Echo*.) A witness.
YASEEN	You can't destroy us.

QAMAR *closes her eyes to calm herself.*

QAMAR One foot, in front of the other.

Second to second.

Minute to minute.

Hour to hour.

Inch by inch.

ACT TWO

Scene One

The memorial wall. QAMAR *is standing at the wall.* STAX *enters.*

STAX	Shouldn't you be at school or something?
QAMAR	It's summer holidays. Where has it gone?

STAX *looks at the blank wall.*

STAX	Where's what gone?
QAMAR	Don't do that –
STAX	Don't do what?
QAMAR	– The painting thingy you did. For Yase–
	– For Dizzy?
STAX	Looks like they buffed it.
QAMAR	Buffed it?
STAX	Got rid of it, yeah.
QAMAR	What do you mean got rid of it?
STAX	I thought it might've been you.
QAMAR	Me?
STAX	You were gonna call the authorities?
QAMAR	That's before I knew –
	– how could they?

STAX *smirks.*

Why are you smirking?

QAMAR *gets in his face.*

STAX	Certain level of irony in this.
QAMAR	How?
STAX	A few days ago, you're filming me, calling me a criminal.
	Now you're acting like they got rid of the *Mona Lisa*.
QAMAR	Well I obviously didn't understand who it was for.
STAX	Yeah, you assumed the worst.
QAMAR	Why are you being a smart arse?
STAX	Give you an example, yeah. Mate of mine in the graff world, blew up 'cause some journalist done a profile on him in *The New York Times* or something. Now he's got some politician called David Lammy belling up his line to buy his 'art' and Banksy's PR team telling how to market himself.
QAMAR	What's your point?
STAX	I'm saying you can go from 'criminal' to artist just like that.
QAMAR	Are you done making this about yourself.
STAX	Jesus, I'm just sayi–
QAMAR	– I don't get how you're so relaxed.
STAX	It got buffed. Happens all the time.
QAMAR	I'm going to apply for a permit.
STAX	You what?
QAMAR	To get it permanently installed.
STAX	Nah, nah, nah.
QAMAR	It won't get removed that way.
STAX	I don't ask, I just do it.

ACT TWO, SCENE ONE 27

QAMAR But that's not how it works.

STAX In my world, we got rules, but it's not the same as yours.

QAMAR So you're just gonna let it get wiped?

STAX You don't get it.

QAMAR I don't get what? 'Cause you want to be a 'rebel,' you don't want to go down the official channels?

STAX You own this building, yeah?

QAMAR Yeah, I'm the world's youngest landlord.

STAX Landlady.

QAMAR That's not a thing –

STAX – You think the powers that be are gonna let us do a lil tag up on the wall of a building we don't own.

QAMAR If it's a person that's passed, they might –

STAX – They might? Am I gonna beg them for crumbs?

QAMAR Well, I'm applying.

STAX Go ahead. But they gotta know that the shit we do for the dead, that's scripture. No one is stopping me. Not no council pencil-pusher. Nobody.

QAMAR And you think that's going to stop them? The council or the police or whoever? That they won't keep wiping him out?

Destroying it. Erasing his memory?

STAX What else am I gonna do? I done the exact same thing when Cal died.

Beat.

QAMAR	Cal?
STAX	Callum, my son.
YASEEN	(*Echo*.) Light up the sky
	– or burn it all down.
	QAMAR *freezes. Beat.*
STAX	You there?
QAMAR	I'm really sorry. I had no idea.
STAX	I done hundreds of throw-ups for him.
QAMAR	Throw-ups?
STAX	Tags, like this one.
QAMAR	Like, illegally? On walls and everything?
STAX	…Yeah. And I'm going do the same for Diz.
QAMAR	Like everywhere?
STAX	Little pebbles all over the city.
	But what I really got my eye on yeah, is the massive wall near Eastway Tower. One big blank canvas.
QAMAR	What's so special about it?
STAX	You can see it from everywhere.
QAMAR	Why doesn't everyone do it then?
STAX	One guy did. Legend in our scene. Redeem.
	But no one else bothers trying 'cause you gotta cross this choppy bridge, get keys to this railway tunnel –
QAMAR	– An actual railway tunnel?
STAX	Decommissioned innit. But that's right under it. You pass the lights and you got one more locked door before you got to climb up 420 steps.

ACT TWO, SCENE ONE

QAMAR — 420? Did you make that number up?

STAX — On my mum's life. It's 250 metres underground to the top of the tower innit. It's some *Lord of the Rings* shit... Tell me you know –

QAMAR — – I read Tolkien when I was thirteen.

STAX — I've only seen the movies.

QAMAR — So you're going to do Eastway Tower?

STAX — Yeah, but I'll need to drag a mate along. You need an extra pair of hands to get it done. Diz and I always made a plan to do it.

STAX and DIZZY. Right up there in the sky.

Beat.

STAX *maps out their names.*

YASEEN — (*Echo.*) Light up the sky?

QAMAR — Light up the sky.

STAX — Yeah, trust.

QAMAR — Maybe I could help.

STAX — With what? A permit?

QAMAR — That extra pair of hands you'll need.

STAX — I know you're Diz's sister, I don't even know your name?

QAMAR — Qamar.

STAX — Like camouflage?

QAMAR — Qa-mar. It means... 'the moon'.

STAX — Look Ka-ma –

– Qam, I don't really take on work experience and that.

QAMAR	What about my brother?
STAX	That was different.
QAMAR	Just this one wall, that's all I'm asking. I'll do whatever you need.
STAX	It's not personal, it's about safety.
QAMAR	Hold on, what's your name?
STAX	Stax.
QAMAR	Stacks? Like pancakes?
STAX	Yeah. Used to be good at Jenga.
QAMAR	Used to be –
	– Look, I really won't be a nuisance.
STAX	Ain't gonna happen.
QAMAR	Feels like sexism.
STAX	I'm not a sexist.
QAMAR	Let me guess, you're going to tell me you're a feminist now –
STAX	I'm not a feminist –
QAMAR	– Excuse you?
STAX	I'm not nothing, okay?
QAMAR	You think girls can't handle it.
STAX	I never said that.
	I can't risk taking someone, girl, boy, whoever. And hold their hand through it.
QAMAR	It would be disturbing if you tried to hold my hand.
STAX	I meant like, having to carry someone –
QAMAR	– Making it worse.

ACT TWO, SCENE ONE 31

STAX — You get my point.

QAMAR — Fine. Fine. Absolutely fine.

STAX — Cool. I'm gonna do right by him, with this burner. You'll see.

QAMAR turns away from STAX. She looks like she's about to cry.

You alright?

Qam?

QAMAR — I just need a minute.

STAX — You sure? Like, I can go?

QAMAR — No, I'll leave.

STAX — Course, course. Do your thing. All love and respect to your family –

QAMAR — – I'll leave.

STAX — – Be safe, yeah –

QAMAR — – And buy class A drugs to cope –

STAX — – What?

QAMAR — And spiral –

STAX — – Listen –

QAMAR — – Into homelessness.

STAX — Hold on –

QAMAR — – Closure isn't for everyone, I guess.

STAX — That's not erm –

QAMAR — – And the one thing that could give me closure, I'm being

DENIED.

STAX — Oh my days.

QAMAR	No, it's fine. It's a risk. You're right.
STAX	You gotta understand where I'm coming from.
QAMAR	Risk to my mental well-being.
STAX	That's not fair –
QAMAR	– 'Cause you're really out here doing up risk assessments every time you do a wall. Makes sense.

STAX *takes a deep breath.*

STAX	I get why you wanna do this, Qam, but I can't be taking a novice to Eastway Tower.

QAMAR *looks annoyed.*

You be safe though, yeah.

STAX *exits.*

Scene Two

Somewhere, someplace. The Axis. The roar of cars in the distance.

YASEEN	*Teta* always called me 'the wanderer'.
QAMAR	You're back?
QAMAR	(*Echo.*) You can't go there.
YASEEN	Says who?
QAMAR	(*Echo.*) Says Baba?
YASEEN	I'll do what I like.
QAMAR	(*Echo.*) You're gonna get me in trouble.
YASEEN	You're the golden child, they won't care.

ACT TWO, SCENE TWO 33

QAMAR   Don't leave.

YASEEN   I'm seeing my mate, you'll be alright, yeah?

QAMAR   (*To herself.*) You're selfish.

YASEEN   I need some breathing space, Qam.

QAMAR   (*Echo.*) Baba and Mama left us alone, you're meant to stay.

YASEEN   I'll only be a few hours –

– a few hours –

STAX   (*Echo.*) I can't be taking a novice to Eastway Tower.

QAMAR   Who?

(*Echo.*) You're selfish.

YASEEN   That hurts, Qam.

QAMAR   I didn't mean that.

YASEEN   Especially coming from you.

STAX   (*Echo.*) And hold their hand through it.

QAMAR   Don't go. I'm asking you not to go.

QAMAR   (*Echo.*) If only you cared about your family. Your little sister.

YASEEN   I'll only be a few hours.

QAMAR   I didn't say that.

YASEEN   A few hours.

QAMAR   I wish I didn't say that.

(*Echo.*) The body of the teenager was found by the British Transport Police.

One foot, in front of the other.

YASEEN   Did they mention I was handsome?

QAMAR	Second to second.
YASEEN	They didn't say I was doing the maddest dub ever, did they?
QAMAR	(*Echo*.) Shortly after eight twenty-two a.m. on the third of June.
	Minute to minute.
YASEEN	The kind of burner you'd see from space.
QAMAR	(*Echo*.) Police have ruled the tragedy an accident and his death currently remains a mystery.
YASEEN	Like this proper mad mix of orange, red and green.
QAMAR	Hour to hour.
YASEEN	A shooting star.
	– or a fiery asteroid.

Scene Three

Halfords. The distant sound of tills. STAX *roams around Halfords,* QAMAR *follows without him noticing.*

STAX *turns around.*

STAX	Jesus, Mary and Joseph. Did you follow me?
QAMAR	No.
STAX	You just happen to be here then?
QAMAR	I needed things.
STAX	What do you need from Halfords?
QAMAR	I needed erm –
	– The motor oil.

STAX	It is a two-for-one to be fair. Bargain.
	You seriously got nothing better to do?
QAMAR	Stax, this is important to me.
	STAX *pauses*.
STAX	Alright. If you're really about this, you gotta listen to me carefully.
QAMAR	I'm an A-star student.
STAX	I'm gonna need you not to argue or question me.
QAMAR	That goes against everything I was taught.
STAX	You wanna do this or not, Qam?
QAMAR	I do, I do.
STAX	Cool, you're gonna grab some paint and you're gonna walk out.
QAMAR	How much is it?
STAX	Don't worry about that.
QAMAR	Do you know how the system of buying and selling works?
STAX	No sarcasm either.
QAMAR	I know you said no questions, but I asked you to teach me how to do graffiti, not to be groomed into being a criminal.
STAX	Firstly, I never agreed to teach you or anyone. You followed me. Secondly, no one is grooming anyone.
QAMAR	You're trying to force a fifteen-year-old to steal.
STAX	Nah, you're just giving up.
	QAMAR *begins to walk off*.

QAMAR	I don't know why I bothered.
STAX	Word of advice though yeah, stop playing the victim.
QAMAR	Who's being a victim?
STAX	Life is rough and tumble. We both lost someone we care about. We both gotta deal with it.
	No point wallowing.
QAMAR	Do you know even know what it's like to feel this crushing guilt –
STAX	– Course I do, I got a bit of Cornish heritage –
QAMAR	– No that's not what I was saying –
STAX	– I get it, you're Muslim and that.
QAMAR	– What's that got to do with anything –
STAX	– Diz even tried to get me into it all.
QAMAR	Into Islam?
STAX	Yeah, well my cousin, lives in Cornwall, converted. Charlie. He was always a bit of an outsider innit 'cause he was ginger and that.
QAMAR	Gingers are the fifth column. Solidarity.
STAX	Trust. But it all went a bit left.
QAMAR	How?
STAX	He went to Syria.
QAMAR	Guessing it wasn't a holiday.
	STAX *shakes his head*.
QAMAR	Cornish convert to ISIS pipeline.
STAX	Happily married though. He's up in Wakefield now.

ACT TWO, SCENE THREE

QAMAR   And Shamima is in a refugee camp.

STAX   Never thought about it like that.

QAMAR   Course you didn't.

STAX   Mind you, I did read the Qur'an. I know some of my *akhs* are shotting class A but never miss *Jummah*.

QAMAR   I don't think that's mentioned in the Qur'an. And I'm also sure that stealing isn't allowed –

STAX   – Yeah, some people say it's *haram*. It's all interpretation 'cause it's about not taking by false means. But if everything gets taken from you by false means then it's all fair game innit.

QAMAR   Did you just drop a *fatwa*.

STAX   Eh? Nah, I didn't fart.

QAMAR   What?

A customer announcement.

VOICEOVER   Would customers be reminded to please return their trolleys to the designated area after purchase.

STAX   We doing this or what?

The announcement jolts QAMAR.

QAMAR   What if I asked for discount?

STAX   It ain't about the money.

QAMAR   I can sign up to their loyalty card?

STAX   Nah, you're gonna take the paint and walk out.

QAMAR   Online delivery?

STAX   Nope.

QAMAR	I have to do this?
STAX	You ain't got a choice.
QAMAR	Excuse me?
STAX	It's a rite of passage.
QAMAR	I don't agree with it.
STAX	Why?
QAMAR	Morally, it's wrong.
STAX	Who you wronging? Halfords?
QAMAR	It's the principle.
STAX	Yeah, it's the principle –
QAMAR	– the principle of stealing? The till is just there.

QAMAR *heads over to the till.*

STAX	Yeah, yeah. Go ahead. But I ain't helping you tag nothing then.

QAMAR *considers her options.*

QAMAR	Fine, I quit.
STAX	You quit?
QAMAR	Yes.

QAMAR *hands* STAX *the paint.*

STAX	That's it then? You given up already, yeah.
QAMAR	Well if it's either that or stealing –
STAX	– Just another NPC then.
QAMAR	Give me a break.
STAX	Your brother, Diz. He was a wolf. And the rest of you are like sheep. And we need you to be the sheep. We need you to follow the rules. Diz used to jump from rooftop to rooftop doing dubs, burners, you name it.

QAMAR	He jumped where?
STAX	He was into parkour innit.
QAMAR	And you led him down this path.
STAX	What path?
QAMAR	Stealing and jumping across dangerous buildings.
STAX	Diz lived for graff.
QAMAR	God knows what you did to him.
STAX	What you talking about?
QAMAR	(*Echo.*) The body of the teenager was found by the British Transport Police.
	QAMAR *takes a deep breath.*
YASEEN	(*Echo.*) Don't tell me you're gonna freeze, Qam?
QAMAR	Yaseen?

Scene Four

Somewhere, someplace. The Axis. The distant sound of tills.

YASEEN	How could I miss you being a baby? As usual.
QAMAR	Just stay here, stay right here.
	QAMAR *closes her eyes.*
QAMAR	Minute to minute.
YASEEN	Baby. A big baby.

Scene Five

Halfords. STAX *is trying to get through to* QAMAR.

STAXHello? We ain't got all day.

Qam? Qamar?

Scene Six

Somewhere, someplace. The Axis. The distant sound of tills.

YASEENAll you do is cry.

QAMAR(*Echo.*) No I don't.

YASEENYou're the spoilt one.

QAMAR(*Echo.*) no, I am not.

YASEENYou ever seen Baba hug me like that?

QAMARCome here, Yas.

YASEENI don't need a hug.

QAMAR(*Echo.*) Ouch. You bit my hand.

YASEEN'Cause you threw my *Match Attax* in the bin. You know how hard it was to get Platinum Messi.

QAMAR(*Echo.*) Because you drew all over my maths book. Put that stupid S all over it.

YASEENThat S is iconic, you're lucky. Blessed.

QAMARI really need you, Yas.

Scene Seven

Halfords. STAX *claps to try get her attention.*

STAX   If you don't stop faffing about, I'm going. I'm done.

Scene Eight

Somewhere, someplace. The Axis. The distant sound of tills.

YASEEN   What's stopping you?

QAMAR   From what?

YASEEN   Living.

QAMAR   Stealing isn't living.

YASEEN   It ain't about stealing.

QAMAR   What is it about?

YASEEN   A mustard seed.

QAMAR   I don't understand.

YASEEN   Taking a leap of faith.

   Beat.

QAMAR   Yas?

YASEEN   Yeah?

QAMAR   I need to ask you something.

QAMAR   (*Echo.*) Second to second.

QAMAR   Did someone push you?

YASEEN   I don't know.

QAMAR	Did you fall?
YASEEN	I don't know.
QAMAR	– Did you jump?
YASEEN	I did.
QAMAR	(*Echo*.) Second to second.
	Did you?
YASEEN	I didn't.
QAMAR	I need to know.
YASEEN	Three.
QAMAR	(*Echo*.) Second to second.
	Stop.
YASEEN	Two.
QAMAR	I asked you a question, Yas.
YASEEN	One.
QAMAR	Yaseen? Don't go.
YASEEN	Remember what I said, yeah?

Scene Nine

Halfords.

STAX	– QAM?
QAMAR	– Yes, yeah.
STAX	Finally, you're with me, yeah?
QAMAR	I'm –
STAX	– On the count of three, I'll leave, yeah. And you count to three, and do the same. We're just strolling out.
QAMAR	I'm not sure I'm fully –

ACT TWO, SCENE NINE

STAX	The more scatty you look, the more you'll stick out.
	One.
QAMAR	Hold on.
STAX	Two.
QAMAR	Stax.
STAX	Three. Qam?

STAX *walks away.*

QAMAR	Do you think he jumped?

STAX *stops.*

STAX	What?
QAMAR	Do you – do you think Yaseen jumped?
STAX	This ain't the time or place.
QAMAR	He didn't leave a note. He didn't say a word. He just left one day and never came back.
STAX	We gotta go. This is looking sus.
QAMAR	It's not logical.
STAX	It never is. Come on.
QAMAR	You spent time with him. You knew what he was going through –
STAX	It ain't for me to –
QAMAR	– ANSWER THE QUESTION. Please. Just answer the question.
STAX	I wasn't there.
QAMAR	You have more answers than I do.

A customer announcement.

VOICEOVER	This is your final store announcement that we are closing the tills in the next two minutes.

STAX	We don't have time.
QAMAR	I don't care.
STAX	I can't give you an answer –
QAMAR	No?
STAX	I don't think he did –
QAMAR	– He might have said something to you.
STAX	Let's go outside.
QAMAR	No.
STAX	Don't be unreasonable.
QAMAR	There is something you're not telling me.
STAX	I haven't got time for this.

STAX *walks away.*

QAMAR	Where were you, the night he fell?
STAX	What do you mean?
QAMAR	It's a simple question.
STAX	What you tryna say?
QAMAR	That you've never given me a straight answer.
STAX	I got nothing to prove to you.
QAMAR	You did something to him, didn't you? You're the one who hurt him?
STAX	That's bullshit.
QAMAR	I think you don't seem to care about anything…
	…even your own son.

Beat.

STAX	I was on fucking curfew, wasn't I? I couldn't be there.

ACT TWO, SCENE NINE   45

I couldn't be there for him. You think I didn't want to?

STAX *leaves*.

QAMAR *follows, An alarm goes off. She freezes*.

Qam, run. RUN.

QAMAR *is frozen*.

QAMAR. RUN. WHAT YOU DOING?

A SECURITY GUARD *starts shouting*.

SECURITY GD   STOP RIGHT THERE.

STAX   LET'S GO.

STAX *runs*. QAMAR *runs after him*.

ACT THREE

Scene One

One week later. The memorial wall. QAMAR, *who has her face covered with a keffiyeh, attempts a tag for* YASEEN. *It's not very good.*

A train above rattles by. QAMAR *takes a moment.* STAX *enters out of view.*

QAMAR	One foot, in front of the other.
	Second to second.
	Minute to minute.
	Hour to hour.
	Inch by inch.
	No sense of rhythm.
STAX	– Not bad.
	QAMAR *is startled.*
	For a seasoned shoplifter.
	STAX *points at the paint.*
QAMAR	It was an accident.
STAX	Can't hear you.
	QAMAR *pulls the keffiyeh down.*
QAMAR	An ACCIDENT.
STAX	Tell that to the judge.
QAMAR	Did you tell the police?
STAX	You think I'm that petty?

QAMAR	You've literally told me how you've gone over other graff writers that disrespect you.
STAX	The game is the game.
QAMAR	There we go.
STAX	This is different. A man has got to have a code.
QAMAR	Only men get codes, interesting.
STAX	Surprised you wanna chat to me since you think I'm a murderer.
QAMAR	That's not what I said.
STAX	Heavily implied.
QAMAR	I've got to finish this.

QAMAR *turns around and shakes the can to continue her tag.*

STAX	Yeah, go ahead.
	Technique is all wrong though.
	You got to go closer.

QAMAR *goes closer to the wall.*

Closer.

And don't be so tense.

QAMAR	You're not a good teacher.

Pause. STAX *cranes his neck to look at her tag.*

STAX	You're a bit like the graff version of Van Gogh. With the paint dripping and that.
QAMAR	You're a prick.
STAX	People would pay to get those kind of comparisons from me.

QAMAR	Haven't you got somewhere to be?
STAX	I just came here to ask if you need my alibi?
	QAMAR *stops spraying*.
	Listen though, yeah, I am s-s-sorry.
QAMAR	What?
STAX	Couldn't give you an answer… about Diz–
	– Yaseen. I beat myself up about –
	– That I couldn't be there.
	– for him –
	– Like physically. You know?
QAMAR	– No, it's –
	– I shouldn't have said what I said about your son –
STAX	– You're good.
	STAX *pauses*.
	Callum was my beautiful boy.
QAMAR	That must've been really –
STAX	– it felt like the end of the world.
	STAX *pauses*.
	You just gotta trust someone enough to pull you out the trenches.
QAMAR	I think I'm fine. In fact, I know I'm fine.
STAX	See, I noticed you go in your head a lot.
QAMAR	I wouldn't say a lot.
STAX	You can always tell.
QAMAR	What do you mean?
STAX	I got lucky. After Cal died, I was off the rails.

ACT THREE, SCENE ONE

	Went to pen and when I got out, I met that guy I told you about, Redeem. Probably saw something in me that was broken. Heard rumours the geezer used to smoke crack and do graff most days, but he seemed sober.
	He used to take me to that tunnel. The one under Eastway Tower. There's little side alley there where you got these fluorescent lights and all this moss.
	Redeem used to tell me to close my eyes and think of him.
QAMAR	Think of Callum?
STAX	Sounds nutty I know, and I ain't even religious or nothing.
	But I tried it.
QAMAR	And?
STAX	...Nothing.
QAMAR	Oh.
STAX	Nah, I'm joking. I saw him. I saw Callum. In 4D. This little skinny kid. With glasses. Fragile but smart like you –
QAMAR	– I'm not fragile.
STAX	He'd probably have applied for Oxford. We didn't always gel.
	But we bonded over graff. Like an awkward alliance. His mum would get jarred that we'd go on these late-night adventures but Cal ended up keeping them a secret. It was like our secret. I'd show him all the places you wouldn't ever see if you lived some sheltered, bullshit nine-to-five life. And the end of the night, he'd always look at me like I'm ten foot tall.

QAMAR	Do you you think he heard you?
STAX	In the Axis? Yeah, definitely.
QAMAR	The Axis?
STAX	That's what I call it.
QAMAR	I don't get how it works –
STAX	– You gotta feel it to believe it –
QAMAR	– But the physics of it?
STAX	– Something to do with ley lines, I reckon.
QAMAR	Ley lines?
STAX	That's my working theory innit.
QAMAR	I've read into it.
STAX	Yeah?
QAMAR	It's pseudoscience.
STAX	Says who?
QAMAR	Reputable physicists.
STAX	You saying I'm going mad then?
QAMAR	I don't mean to be skeptical –
STAX	– I don't go round shouting about it but I came here, 'cause I thought it might actually help you. Maybe that was pointless.
QAMAR	I want to believe it exists, I do.
STAX	I paint on walls, 'cause that's what's real. But it's not always enough. So each time I'm doing a burner or a dub for them, or for me. I'm thinking each second could be a lifetime. Imagine, they're up there, smiling and watching millions of lifetimes by the time I've done up just one wall.

Beat.

QAMAR	I think the more time passes, the more I'm losing him.
STAX	Yaseen?
QAMAR	I used to be able to hold onto him, now it feels like he's sliding into nothingness. It's like that light –
	– That light has gone somewhere else.
STAX	Maybe you haven't lost him.
QAMAR	What do you mean?
STAX	I know you think it's all bollocks, but if you wanna say goodbye, we should go say goodbye innit.

Scene Two

Wicksteed Bridge. STAX *waits for* QAMAR.

On the other side, QAMAR *silently raises her hands to do dua.*

QAMAR *enters.*

STAX	What you doing?
QAMAR	I was praying –
STAX	What? That BTP don't come? You see the cameras?
QAMAR	Lots of them.
STAX	Why'd you look stressed?
QAMAR	We are about to do something very illegal.
STAX	We got the most surveillance in the world. And now the feds got facial recognition and that.

QAMAR	Is that supposed to make me feel better?
STAX	We'll be fine.
QAMAR	Should I be worried that you're on tag?
STAX	Minor offences.
QAMAR	Like?
STAX	This and that, you know?
QAMAR	No, I don't?
STAX	At a certain point, I was getting bagged for just walking round with paint.
QAMAR	Great, I'm working with a convicted felon.
STAX	I always say, you got a break one law a day.
	Alright, we gotta cross this bridge thing to get to that tunnel.
	Takeshi's Castle ting.
QAMAR	*Takeshi's* what?
STAX	You ain't seen it? I used to watch it on acid.
	Alright cool, all we need is a key, hold tight.
	STAX *searches for the key in his tote bag*.
QAMAR	Thank God the weather isn't too bad.
STAX	Thank Allah, my good sis.
QAMAR	Very funny.
STAX	Bruv, where has this key gone?
QAMAR	How did you even get this key?
STAX	Got a mate called Munaj. Bengali guy. I call him Mad Muj. Lives in Tower Hamlets, you can see the Barclays building from his yard. He shots coke. Said his number one clients are all judges and MPs. Anyway, his ex used

ACT THREE, SCENE TWO

	to work for TfL. And she was operations manager for this site. So he got with her on a rebound and nicked the keys for me as a favour.
QAMAR	That's quite a big favour you pulled.
STAX	I helped him out in the past.
QAMAR	Kind of you to help out your drug-dealer friend.
STAX	That's how we got the HS2 key, got through the asbestos underpass to this bridge.
QAMAR	You skimmed past that whole asbestos thing.
STAX	We'll be fine, it's like, you need a bit of that to improve your immune system.
QAMAR	That's not how it works –
	STAX *tips the contents of the tote bag on the floor, there is a Vaseline, large headphones and some spray cans, he finds the key.*
STAX	Here we go.
	STAX *takes a key and tries to jam open the door.*
QAMAR	You alright there?
STAX	He said this would work.
QAMAR	Let me try.
STAX	Nah, it's quite solid innit. You might struggle.
	QAMAR *takes the key and opens the door with ease.*
QAMAR	Women in STEM.
STAX	What's STEM?
	STAX *walks toward the door.*
	You coming or what?

QAMAR	You go ahead, it's okay.
STAX	It ain't some pagan-ritual thing, don't stress.
QAMAR	I think I've changed my mind.
STAX	Qam?
QAMAR	No, I actually think I'm at peace with it.
STAX	I really dunno about that. Looks like a whole lot of chaos under that.
QAMAR	That's racist.
STAX	I meant in your head.
QAMAR	I'll head back.
STAX	You got this far, the Axis ain't far now.
QAMAR	It's not about the distance –
STAX	– You already crossed the bridge?
QAMAR	Like you said, you can't take a novice with you.
STAX	You know what's mad.
QAMAR	What?
STAX	That your older brother followed me too.
QAMAR	Yas followed you?
STAX	Kid was doing parkour at two a.m.
QAMAR	He used to stress out Mama and Baba.
STAX	I was doing a burner in the middle of the night, alone.

Scene Three

Somewhere, someplace. The Axis. QAMAR *is disturbed by* YASEEN*'s voice.*

YASEEN   I clocked him straight away. This man with a bally doing up the maddest painting. Like a roadman Picasso. It wasn't just the tag. It's the way his arm was flowing. Effortless.

                Next thing, I clocked a bully van, I end up shouting, 'THE FEDS, RUN.' My guy sprints like Usain.

QAMAR   Yaseen?

YASEEN   I dunno what made me run after him, but I did. Chased him down these side streets, he was baffled. But weirdly impressed. That's when I said…

                …I wanna do what you do.

STAX   (*Echo.*) 'I wanna do what you do.'

Scene Four

Wicksteed Bridge.

STAX   Mad story innit?

QAMAR   Did you hear that?

STAX   Hear what?

QAMAR   His voice?

STAX   Probably 'cause we're getting close.

QAMAR   No, no way?

STAX	You thought I was chatting shit, innit.
	QAMAR *freezes.*
	You coming or what?

Scene Five

Under the Eastway Tower, in a decommissioned tunnel, the Axis.

STAX	Here we go. This is it. This is the place.
	QAMAR *looks around in wonder.*
QAMAR	The Axis.
STAX	I'll be outside, yeah.
QAMAR	What, w-w-hy?
STAX	I said I wouldn't hold your hand through it, didn't I?
QAMAR	But how do I –
	– How does it even?
STAX	– Don't be long 'cause we gotta do this Dizzy burner, yeah?
	STAX *exits.*
QAMAR	Stax, wait.
	QAMAR *takes a moment. She closes her eyes. A sudden sonic whirlwind of the sirens, the sounds of tills, cars roaring past and trains rattling by.*
	One foot, in front of the other.
	Second to second.
	Minute to minute.
YASEEN	No sense of time.

ACT THREE, SCENE FIVE

QAMAR	Yaseen?
YASEEN	What took you so long, Qam?
QAMAR	He wasn't lying.
YASEEN	Who wasn't?
QAMAR	Stax.
	YASEEN *laughs*.
YASEEN	Old Uncle Stax. I thought he was some nitty at first, then I thought he might be crazy, then I think damn, maybe he's a *wali* or suttin.
QAMAR	I don't know about that.
YASEEN	He told me about all these patterns, you know.
QAMAR	I wish you told me what you were doing, Yas.
YASEEN	You think I knew myself? I was on some aimless ting.
QAMAR	I didn't even know your tag, now I'm seeing Dizzy everywhere.
YASEEN	I got about. Guest booking.
QAMAR	On the trains, on walls, on bus stops, in tunnels.
YASEEN	Those felt like endless days, I swear.
QAMAR	Everywhere is a reminder.
YASEEN	I was ACTIVE. Unique style and that.
QAMAR	You could've been an artist.
YASEEN	I was, Qam.
QAMAR	You could've been anything you wanted.
YASEEN	I was everything I needed to be.
QAMAR	Now I've finally got you, you're really here. You're really here, right?
	QAMAR *breaks down*.

YASEEN	Qam, I'll be here when you need to reach for me innit.
QAMAR	In the Axis?

Pause.

YASEEN	Nah, I'll tell you where I'll be.
QAMAR	I need to know.
YASEEN	You know them Northern Lights you see in Norway and that?
QAMAR	What? Once in a blue moon?
YASEEN	Nah I'm saying I'd be like them particles hitting magnetic poles. When you get these mad colours in the sky.
QAMAR	I don't understand.
YASEEN	I'll always be floating about like a –
	– like a fiery asteroid.
QAMAR	Or a shooting star.
YASEEN	Exactly.
QAMAR	If the universe has ten trillion galaxies and one hundred billion stars, maybe you're one of the youngest ones. One of the bravest ones. One that I saw and loved.
YASEEN	Won't be hard to find me.
QAMAR	If I could tell you how much Baba and Mama are hurting.
YASEEN	Can't fix that now, but I will… eventually.

Pause.

I was thinking, maybe I do understand algebra.

QAMAR	You do?

YASEEN's voice starts to fade.

YASEEN	*Al-Jabr*, the reunion of broken parts.
QAMAR	What do I do, Yaseen?
YASEEN	Just keep spraying, you'll be alright.
QAMAR	I won't let them destroy you.
YASEEN	They never will, Qam.
	I want you to go do the maddest burner, yeah?

Scene Six

Eastway Tower wall. The roar of cars from below. STAX *is waiting for* QAMAR.

QAMAR *arrives and is out of breath.*

QAMAR	You did make that number up!
STAX	You counted each step?
QAMAR	422 individual stairs. No more, no less.
STAX	I prefer 420.
QAMAR	I wonder why.
STAX	Oi, don't drug-shame me.
QAMAR	I'm not.
STAX	I thought your generation are meant to be proper open and that.
	QAMAR *looks around. The distant sound of cars below.*
	Everything go alright down there?
	QAMAR *nods.*
	Everyone's got their own one. Mad innit.
QAMAR	Their own Axis?

STAX: Yeah, you just gotta make sure you don't get stuck in it when you visit.

Beat.

Did I ever tell you your brother saved my life?

QAMAR: No?

STAX: We were doing one of the big freight trains. It was a risky dub 'cause I'd be on live tracks. I needed Diz to be the lookout.

I knew I had two minutes to do a dub that would take me one minute.

We got up at dawn. One of them sunny but cold days.

Got to the train yard, Diz flew over like a gazelle.

So here we are, about to put the plan in action. Back then, I'd have this habit of putting my headphones on.

Nas – 'Whose world is this?' Volume up. Boom, I start. Now I'm in the flow. No one can stop me. Diz is above looking out for security or trains.

I had no clue, that that morning, they changed up the train schedules.

But I couldn't hear Diz screaming at the top of his lungs telling me to move. NO CLUE. I look left. I see this massive freight train heading my way. All I feel is two hands pull me up. It all happened in a few seconds.

Like BAM. I can hear the whir of the train. I'm dizzy. Gone. I see Diz on his back, breathless. Tears in his eyes. Fuck, I started crying too. And we hugged. We hugged for a little while. 'Cause shit. That could've been it.

ACT THREE, SCENE SIX   61

QAMAR   That's wild.

STAX   Trust me.

Pause.

Your brother was a good guy, Qam. It could've been an accident, he could've slipped. I don't think he jumped.

But I wouldn't have blamed him if he did, it don't take away from who he was.

Beat.

QAMAR   Some days, it feels impossible.

STAX   I tell myself, just keep spraying, you'll be alright.

QAMAR   That's strange?

STAX   What is?

QAMAR   I feel like I've heard that before?

STAX   Maybe I'm one of them saints.

QAMAR   I highly doubt it.

STAX *laughs.*

I've been thinking about Pi a lot.

STAX   Me too. You gotta try Deano's Pie and Mash.

QAMAR   The mathematical equation.

STAX   Oh right, yeah?

QAMAR   Even the smartest minds in the worlds are blown away by it.

Because it's a constant stream of numbers that never ends.

And then you got all these theories that stem from it, like Wave Theory. And I thought, maybe we're made up of atoms that orbit each other.

STAX	– Like invisible string theory. I went on some five-hour YouTube rabbit hole about this one night.
QAMAR	I thought that maybe Yaseen and Callum are like those atoms in orbit, and that was our time with them.
STAX	That's some fourth-dimension shit. Redeem used to say that about graff.
QAMAR	What would he say?
STAX	One minute it's there and the next it's not. It's mad fragile.
	Best thing we can do is pay attention while it's here innit. 'Cause it might not be there tomorrow. Like this atom shit you're talking about.
QAMAR	'I, a universe of atoms, an atom in the universe.'
STAX	Mad, is that Shakespeare?
QAMAR	No. Just some physicist.
STAX	A reputable physicist, yeah?
QAMAR	Shut up.
	Pause.
STAX	Come, we doing this massive burner on the wall then?
QAMAR	Next to Redeem's dub?
STAX	One hundred.
	They both walk toward the Eastway Tower wall.
QAMAR	We got to make sure it all lines up.
STAX	You got a spirit level?

QAMAR	Is that graff terminology?
STAX	Nah, it's – never mind.
QAMAR	Okay. Fifteen by fifteen wall, so each letter should be roughly four metres and –
STAX	– Don't overthink it, I got you.
QAMAR	You're right, Stax.
STAX	Call me Sunny.
QAMAR	Sunny?
STAX	It's my government name, but my real ones call me that.
QAMAR	Thanks, Sunny.
STAX	You wanna do the honours then?

STAX *hands her the paint.*

Remember, it's like doing massive Wotsits.

Dizzy Forever?

QAMAR How about, Dizzy. 4 Eva?

QAMAR *and* STAX *tag the Eastway Tower Wall together.*

End.

A Nick Hern Book

Dizzy first published in Great Britain in 2024 as a paperback original by Nick Hern Books Limited, The Glasshouse, 49a Goldhawk Road, London W12 8QP, in association with Theatre Centre and Sheffield Theatres

Dizzy copyright © 2024 Mohamed-Zain Dada

Original artwork copyright © 2024 Cherry Bee

Mohamed-Zain Dada has asserted his moral right to be identified as the author of this work

Cover image: Rebecca Pitt

Designed and typeset by Nick Hern Books, London
Printed in the UK by Mimeo Ltd, Huntingdon, Cambridgeshire PE29 6XX

A CIP catalogue record for this book is available from the British Library

ISBN 978 1 83904 395 6

CAUTION All rights whatsoever in this play are strictly reserved. Requests to reproduce the text in whole or in part should be addressed to the publisher.

Amateur Performing Rights Applications for performance, including readings and excerpts, by amateurs in the English language throughout the world should be addressed to the Performing Rights Department, Nick Hern Books, The Glasshouse, 49a Goldhawk Road, London W12 8QP, *tel* +44 (0)20 8749 4953, *email* rights@nickhernbooks.co.uk, except as follows:

Australia: ORiGiN Theatrical, Level 1, 213 Clarence Street, Sydney NSW 2000, *tel* +61 (2) 8514 5201, *email* enquiries@originmusic.com.au, *web* www.origintheatrical.com.au

New Zealand: Play Bureau, 20 Rua Street, Mangapapa, Gisborne, 4010, *tel* +64 21 258 3998, *email* info@playbureau.com

United States and Canada: Casarotto Ramsay and Associates Ltd, see details below

Professional Performing Rights Applications for performance by professionals in any medium and in any language throughout the world (including by stock companies in the USA and Canada) should be addressed to Casarotto Ramsay and Associates Ltd, *email* rights@casarotto.co.uk, www.casarotto.co.uk

No performance of any kind may be given unless a licence has been obtained. Applications should be made before rehearsals begin. Publication of this play does not necessarily indicate its availability for amateur performance.

www.nickhernbooks.co.uk/environmental-policy